The LEAVES on the TREES

Written by
Thom Wiley

Illustrated by
Andrew Day

Cartwheel
·B·O·O·K·S·®

SCHOLASTIC INC.

New York   Toronto   London   Auckland   Sydney   Mexico City   New Delhi   Hong Kong

The **leaves** on the trees are . . .

falling down,

      falling down,

           falling down.

The leaves on the trees
are falling down.
Autumn is here!

The sweet gum leaves turn orange and red, orange and red, orange and red.

The sweet gum leaves turn orange and red. Autumn is here!

The **tulip** leaves turn **green** to gold,
green to gold, **green** to gold.

The
tulip leaves turn
green to gold.
Autumn is here!

The gingko leaves are shaped like fans, shaped like fans, shaped like fans.

The gingko
leaves are shaped
like fans.
Autumn is here!

The maple leaves are colorful!
Colorful! Colorful!

The **maple** leaves are colorful! Autumn is here!

The linden leaves are shaped like hearts,
shaped like hearts, shaped like hearts.

The linden leaves are shaped like hearts. Autumn is here!

The **ash** tree branch has tiny leaves,
tiny leaves, tiny leaves.

The ash tree branch has tiny leaves.

Autumn is here!

The hickory leaves
float on the pond,
on the pond,
on the pond.

The **hickory** leaves float on the pond. Autumn is here!

The sassafras leaves
look like dinosaur tracks!
Dinosaur tracks!
Dinosaur tracks!

The sassafras
leaves look
like dinosaur tracks!
Autumn is here!

The **birch** leaves glow a bright yellow!
Bright yellow! Bright yellow!

The **birch** leaves glow a bright yellow!